Solitude...

Samrat Mukherji

INDIA • SINGAPORE • MALAYSIA

ISBN 979-8-89322-288-3

Dedication

To
my grandmother
who
was
the lighthouse
in my life.

Contents

Contents

Acknowledgement

Within apparent contradictions and complexities lies the beauty of one's life. Life may bring us to face challenges whether existing or contingent. We live a life worth-living while facing those dire threats Undaunted and merely survive if we start cowering under it's spectre. This collection of poems has emerged out of the experience and journey life has taken me through. It has helped me to unravel celestial and terrestrial world; showed me shining days and gloomy nights. My past has seized upon me and a future has beckoned. This humble collection is a mélange of all the queer feelings, thoughts, hopes, despair, anger and fear.

This manuscript for this book would not have been possible but for unstinting support of Sujit Dutta, Anirban Nandy who have worked untiringly to bring the book about.

I deeply acknowledge and admire the encouragement of Sri Ranjit Roy, journalist and Dr. Ramesh Chandra Mukhopadhyaya a doyen of underground literature movement who has lent me a new vision while explicating my poems as elucidated in 'Me and my musing'. All their support and wisdom has helped me to complete this endeavour.

– **Samrat Mukherji**

Prologue

The gateway of mystery is open ajar and the mood of the poetry wavers and alters. They sometime echoes the noiseless noise of silence and sometime depicts torrid human existence. From passionate love to seething desire to disgust to depression to dismay and evoke subtle feeling both strangeous and pleasanter. Some poetry are melancholic while some are gaiety. A deep sense of sorrow and loneliness, dream and delirium imbue the bevy of poems. Each of the poems arouse distinct and disparate mood and feeling on our emotional plane leaving us delighted, bemused and at times saddened. Dreams that excite one's subconscious and transcendence of inner self has deeply moved and influenced my poetry. A fervour of mystery covers each of the poems and vaguely alludes to the thought it tries to convey. Poems like *"no more I wander"*, *"mystic silhouette"* engender a deep and profound love for nature with an underlying message for protecting dear nature from hostile eye. *'Bygone days'* takes us back to the days we left behind and uncovers trove of indelible memory that outlast everything through vicissitude of life.

The vagaries of life laden with woe and our captive helpless existence in present political and social milieu is echoed in *"they born, breed and die"*; a rising ascendancy of religious intolerance is writ large In the poem *'who would dare'* when *'milky way in the sky'* militates against sleeping and slumber. The poems are melange of diverse moods, reflection and emotion.

The book reflects on our feelings, emotion, dilemma and resolute forged by challenges to survival, and vulnerability of existence. There are a couple of narrative poetry which elucidate after life phenomenon enfolded in mystery. An effusive elegy of nature's beauty and its' enigmatic vivacity are brimming in the poems. The book also sketches the dullness and tedium of city life and its urbane aridity through words and imageries befitting to convey the impression.

Distant Lore

No more I wander
On the mountain steps
through the sinuous ways of woods;
For I can still see from here
The crowning popler swaying
And the shadow of passing cloud
swaddling the hills

I can hear the windy
evening shrill
through boughs and overgrown bush
breaking in a flowery hues.

The dark, deep lake
glimmering in moonlit night,
And the silkening stream
shuffling and rustling
In glade.

Solitude

Let no mortal eyes
fall on
the contour of beauty
Unravelling itself in the
In the loneliness of night
For men has murderous eyes
Who invade like unknown aliens.

Awakening of Stars

Milky way in the dark
Treads the nights sky
And a gleaming moon
With brownish eye
Gazes upon the earth.
Sparkling stars
Spangling in dark
Deck up the night.
Aye, don't put the quite astir
Let the night sway
Keeping worldly hustle at bay
Let us shatter the sleep
Only the wind sweep
Over the rugged terrain of my land
Raising a roar amongst swaying trees
Where kindling flame of vengeance once seduced rebellion
Murmuring the love poems of furious passion
And burnt us both.

I Stand Between

I stand between the azure of sky

and blue of your eyes

Dripping with the relentless rain of colours

Soaked with your smell

that the morning breeze brings

And I dream you

agleam…

Far above the hills…

Rises the shimmering landscape

Draped in drifting shades

Of light and cloud

Divine, as your unfurling bosom

Sojourn, to the fallen,

Broken hearts

To rest

In quietude.

Elicitation

Mystic silhouette of dreams
Enthralling, garbed in vibrant hues of colours,
It writes in the void of evening sky
A woeful tale
Of our time.

The sky is in autumn beauty
Brimming lake mirrors the face of city
Paths are dry
Embroidered by fallen leaves

At the daybreak,
The glimmering moon
Vestured in cloud
Hangs over the city,
Still wrapped in slumber
Unruffled by chaotic clamour.

The morning rays
Falls in the humble room, uncluttered
Lights and shades dances on the window pane
A trivial sight becomes joy for ever.

Pain That Blossomed

I am wandering
On desolate ways
In the sheer heat,
Under a flaming sun
Beating down
the endless street.

Eerie evening shade into
Weary nights
of forlorn pain
And wound of unrequited love hurts,
Waking me up to past.

The longing soul
Drowns all the slog and drudgery
In the worn out glass
Of a solitary inn.

The burning bliss trickles
blurring all astir and unquiet
Of a toiled heart
In the still of
the lengthening night.

Samrat Mukherjee

I am shuddered
At her weird footsteps
She stalks on my sleep
like nightmare
In a deserted castle

Dreams tumble over
Dream
In the wilderness of heart.
I stitch and unstitch
My dishevelled thoughts
Of pain, thorn
Mist and rain,
My longing and pities
In the string of
Woeful poetry.

Weary Dreams

I am shrouded by rain
Shining silvery wind blows.
The moon's glimmering gold
with blighted eyes…
gazes upon the earth;
And there I lie… buried under
Your tousled hair
with my eyes
worn with dreams…

Aching of A Longing Soul

The doors flung open
And I still stare
At your path,
through the fading mist
Of parting winter.
My room is heavy
With the chivalrous
Smell of smoke
Wafting from smoldering fire of your lips
And a headier odour
Of cocktail drinks
hovers, as fleeting
shadow
Of an elusive dream.

I have hidden my brittled ribs
In the desert of a wounded heart
Under the tattered quilt,
In the
gloom of bleeding
Night.

Conjuring

Sickly, trembling fingers invades my dream
In the height of sleep
When the lights burns out
And glowing flame dies out
Between my beating heart-throbs she stood.

Darkling intrudes in the nighty silence, unstirred
From the dreamy depth
Awakes the forlorn, forgotten past
And the cry of falling star
Comes faintly from distance.

Frightful unseen and unknown faces
May be some of them I vaguely know
Shrieking out at me wild, untamed
For the answers I did always owe.

Decadence

Who would dare
To tell the truth?
The sun is hiding
And the pale moon would sink.

In the smoky corner of allies
discontents gather;
Under the shedding light of every street lamps
I pass,
Unfallible questions hover
And flutters in the wind
Like indignant desert bird
restless in the night.

Who dares
To tell the truth
Only the lone boy
Who scavenge for food
Would cry and shout
Why so much blood in the street?
Why the face of God would fright?
The questions reverberate around!

Solitude

But I can see nothing
Behind the eye of the
little boy
Does his scream stir the sky?

The question echoes in the shadowy reaches of city's slum
Flaming red
In the fire of blazing faith;
And God fell defeated,
Captivated in a darken
grim temple
where flag of faith
flutters in disdain.

The angel
in hurtling spear
is preaching a
Sermon of vengeance…

Living In The Ruins

Here it rains all the year
Flock of cloud sails across the ravaged land
and throttled river,
That follows a sinuous trail
Through bruised landscape
bearing burnt of human hatred.

The shrill of rain
evokes the mystic pain
When the strain of your song comes
faintly from distance.

In an innocent bliss
I fall asleep
In your arm
In the midst of a pain
boring deep into my heart.

Let the darkness drops
And all worldly compassion

Take refuge under its
widening wings; shedding
ineffable kindness.
Let all pretension and façade shatter
And the soul find its solace
In candid confession.

Transitioning

Silently, on the stony ground, littered
The pyre smoulders;
Where his father lies in a perfect still
Awaiting to be transfigured.

Dear and beloved
Started trickling in
Sobbing, weeping
They stand in a ring;
Some rues and some
Praise for all good done
Which shall only live on.

Does anything linger or live?
Does father really ever die?
He muses gazing at the Alight pyre
Wiping tear from his eye.

The blazing flame
Embrace and burns

The mortal limbs.
Burning and gutting
to the hilt
It stops
Where the dead's heart is

Solitude

The whoosh of fire
Incants sermons
In its crackle and muttering
Whispering unknown hymn.

Months and year saunters
And the tedious river meanders
Over the charred reminiscence of memory.

People embark
And disembark
In perpetual succession
And death and dream blossom and gather.

In the billowing smoke,
A fleeting visage of your face appears.
Beyond the blurring vision
You pass into the mystery-dimmed land
Through the sacred corridor
Forged by the cremating fire;
Soaring slowly, withering high
Free from fallacious riddle
of being born and die.

Captivated

They born, breed and die captive
In the void of monstrous trawl;
And wander within the transient prison
In an ancient locomotion.

Piteous creatures
Finning their weary flippers
In the perilous deep of blue
Where stillness of heart looms
And delusions brew.

The eerie abyss, incites hulking illusion
Blurring out all watery vision.
And the fateful time
Stalks every drifting calculation.

Pitiably they look in a remorseless candour
Deceived and tricked,
and unfazed by the fright and plunder;
Through the dreadful silence they subsist.

Solitude

An unescapable confine
In unworldly depth of sea
conjures darkness
and past losses its memory.

The silvery harvest
Play in a foolish glee
And live to die
With burnt out eye
and dreams are dumped
On the smudge of sea.

Fleetingly they swim
as lurking shadow,
Blissfully unaware of the slaughter
Before the bloody and sudden end
In hunter's spear.

Tears of Rain

And the sky
ripped suddenly apart
from end to end
to bless me
with an unbound torrent
Of rain and thunder
to find the earth verdant once more…

And thus my prayers were answered,
I thought,
But were they in real?
The barren heart bore the happiness of the bloom
Minding itself that the days are there
For me to gloom
Let it rain, I said
And flood the earth with happy drizzles and green and pink
And yellow
My heart will be left dry, I know
Do I care anymore?
My pain would rain
In a shower
In a torrent of unbound tears.

Adrift

If I travel
Someday again
I will travel
In the autumn.
How easy it is
To drift away
Upstream,
Without stirring
The river's quiet;
As if the course
takes me to you.
How easy it is to be
Stripped of all urban hypocrisy
Surrendering to the true desire
Of heart.
The morning sun is brighter
At the day
Shinning on the ruffle of water
And the ripple;
Though it burns my eyes

and destiny eludes me as ever;
Happily I will sink into a swoon
Wishing my drifting ship
Shall never moor
For the ecstasy of your dream
Will fade out
When we will make tryst.

Rain In Twilight

Slowly the rain falls
Drip by drip
And a thin drizzle of words sets in.
It falls in flickering drop
fades and Dissolves.
Uninhibited it falls
From the invisible past;
droplet of tears and laughter
of love and unloved.
Sad evening descends
On the wings of
the weary bird;
A tide of passion is loosed
Stirring up the stillness of heart.

Winter stillness

The winter dawn
Shrouded and pale
A nip in the air
Perceptible;
The hesitating sun shivering
dither to show up
over the leaf-less branches
Stiff and white,
Standing shrivelled
like freaky witches.

City's street wrapped
In an magnificent mist
Though dull and grey
And the fading rays of lamps
Recede,
In the gutter
and in the slum
behind half lighted street
lying in a slumber.

Solitude

The frozen roads
Stretches like tedious existence
through the crowding city-scrapper
And darken allies,
Veiled in vapoury smoke
And staggers
Into an urbane silence.

Platitudes

My morning breaks
In the sputtering
Of radio
That starts muttering
After a little tuning;
And a stirring music
Would follow.
And then a voice
Deep and sombre
Wakes me up
To our leaders daring's do;
How gamely they
played politics
Whenever any trouble grew.
Where did bridge collapse
How was the airplane
Grounded;
There the farmers revolted
And the tribal girl
Outraged.

Solitude

Some nonchalant spook reads
Eyeless, earless
Only obliged to disseminate
rusty information
With a prosaic utterance.

Undaunted

The raging storm
takes us over
We may survive
and can succumb
to its fury!

Shimmering island
dotting the sea
Will sink
Under the swelling waves
In a rash.

They will grapple
With the monstrous upsurge
for a while
And then sink.

Roaring and rumbling
The whirlwind
Sweeps me away
Plunging into a gyring darkness.

Solitude

Inside, everything hurtle down
In a torrent;
Ominous dark cloud
gathers overhead
Portending imminent end;
But I stand unafraid
Let the storm befall
My heart won't tremble,
For I am forged in your fury
And I will stand undeterred.

My Unkind Lover

You caught me ahold
Before I stumble;
Proffered your hanky
to wipe my eye,
before I knew
they would make me cry.

You could hear me
Though nowhere
Around;
and listened to my aching heart;
Darkening thoughts
All my musing, brooding and mulling
Were communed
Sans words.

You strum my pains
In sweeping fingers
to make music
Out of me
In the cruel concert.
Turning my whimper
Into a symphony.

Fossil of Memory

Bygone days
are lost in a muse
with swarming memories.
Moon and stars of past
buried as an uncovered fossil
Under the sand of time,
by the sparkling stream.
And I am lost
In a reverie.

The summer would come here
In purple and yellow
Winter left the stream asleep
Under delightful snow
Far in the distance
On the edge of river
Windy air stumbled
On the storm-broken stairs
And the lonely bridge
Sighed in despair.

By the grey sands of the shallow stream
Ceaseless memories come flooding

And we grow old and worn
day by day
Only memory linger
by the endless river
and one by one
We drop away.

Immersion

Long after you bid an adieu
Long after you have left and gone
After the cries and laughter hushed in silence
The city streets turns quite and clam

The threaded flies blinking
sadly stop kindling
Only the towering pandals lonely stand
as you have left them bare;
Oh mother.
Your benign eyes would still stare
And a poignant memory would linger
In the rustling stream
of a withering autumn
On the bank of an immersing river.

Me and My Musing

Nothing exists unless the so called nothing interacts with something else. This is the latest physics. And the poem entitled 'I stand between' puts forward an emergent aesthetics. The poet stands between the yore of the blue deep and the blue eyes of the addressee. Unless the interaction between the skies and the eyes neither might be there. The time is morning. The mellowing morning breeze is the quinquereme that carries the freight of the fragrance of the addressee. The environment is soaked in sensuousness. Here poetry fails and falters to describe but evokes. And consequently there is a rain of hues. This is the physical side of the environment. A poet is but a human being who cannot be carried off by sensuousness. The photons of the agleam of the addressee charge the poet with a dream. In fact poetry has a kinship with dream. While dreams do not have a transport, poetry is always a dream transported with the aid of language. And the poet is being carried off far above the hills draped in the drifting shades of light and cloud. Here is a chiaroscuro reminiscent of the impressionists. The light and shade of the chiaroscuro sojourn to the fallen broken hearts to rest in quietude. The world is weltering in the waters of untold woe. Batters of gun and shatters of flying muscles in the hurly burly conjured by Hamas — the world is too much with us getting and spending. And here in this context light and cloud and divine sojourn doubtlessly weighs to soothe the broken hearts. In the context of Indian philosophy the worldly life is as such the veritable vision of boundless woe. The Paradise

Lost seems to have portrayed the worldly life laden with woe as it were in the baroque style. It reminds one of the Inferno of Dante. But one wonders whether the poetry lifts us to the heights of the lion gates of heaven where Beatrice the blessed damozel's eyes are gleaming. The poem invokes summer's showers upon the sunburnt heath of our world.

One of the finest physicists of our time Carlo Rovelli in his 'The order of time' observes that the world is made of events, not things. The Milky Way in the dark treads the night sky. The night sky surely stands for Dark Matter that is beyond the ken of humankind. Ironically enough a gleaming moon with brownish eye gazes upon the earth. Opposites interact with each other and lays bare the contradictions and vacillations of human heart. To be or Not to be is the question now. The musing portrays the world as shrouded in darkness with stars swinging from unknown and unknowable infinitude as it were and they might lift mortals and reach them to the doors of heaven. The world about us is as it were a jocund fair or a carnival where a bevy of fairies are bathing in light and sport. The poet asks the sparkling stars spangling in dark decking the night not to put the quiet astir. He tells the night that it had better keep the worldly hassle at bay. The poet asks the Milky Way and Cynthia the spirit of moon to sleep awhile. The poet counsels them— let us sleep. With the advent of slumber the readers as well as the world might forget the weariness of existence. In a sleep walking scene reminiscent of Shakespeare's Macbeth, the poet could hear as it were in a swoon roar among swaying trees where kindling flame of vengeance that once seduced rebellion. It might remind one of the great freedom struggle reeking in our Mother India.

Solitude

And dear readers mark you every rebellion be it in the rugged terrain of my land implies the murmurs of the love poems of furious passion. This is the heat sine qua non with entropy that burns us both the poet and the reader. Unless there is heat there cannot be the entropy and transformation.

They are born, they breed and die captivated, silvery, shining and gleaming prey in the depth of blue where stillness of heart looms in the void of the monstrous trawl. Is this the summing up of existence teeming with myriads of life? The mazarine music is heard where stillness of heart looms in the void of the monstrous trawl. Who preys on all things both great and small? All life merges with the sunless sea. Dust thou art dust returnest. That is the highest voice that reverberates in the realm of nothing. It is the void that lurks behind the show of things. In the all compassing silence, we hear the voice of the monstrous trawl. The word trawl implies search for something priceless. It is as it were pulling a large net that catches everything whatever is precious. Consequentially we can hear the noiseless noise of silence. Is he all ears to the Om or the silence or the motion and the spirits that impels all thinking things and all objects of all thoughts and rolls through all things? The poem tries to sum up all life in an imagery of drifting and dazzling creatures gullible. Why gullible? Because they can be easily tricked with the net of desire, anger, lust and illusion. They are all entrapped in a severed water in the perennial sea of death. They live to die with burnt out eyes blissfully unaware of slaughter in the hand of prying hunter. Who could be the hunter? Since every living thing, be it a man or a beast or a micro organism, is gullible heedless to detect death that steals into the Nature, death awaits them with icy hands to embrace and the rest is silence. It is a pity that we live to die with burnt out eyes blissfully unaware of slaughter before the bloody and sudden end in the hand of prying hunter.

The poem has been composed long after the addressee had left and gone. The consequences have been dismal. The cheers and laughters have been hushed into silence. Silence is as such sine qua none with any speech whatever. The silence or a stop of any discourse might remind the hearer of the hurry that characterise our day to day life plunged in activity and its bustling environment. The physicist might know Heisenberg's notion of indeterminacy. Nothing is at rest. The movement of any electron whatever cannot be predicted. If one seeks to find out its speed, its location is unknown and unknowable. Hence the scientists as well tell us that any absence whatever baffles all possible interpretation. Every event whatever in this existence, be it an accident or an act of God baffles an explanation. We can only detect the glow worms extinguished. In other words the glimmer that might lead one across the roads of life is no longer there. It is impenetrable darkness all over. We are very much a resident of a city like Calcutta where pandals crowd. But we might guess from the pandals that the poem has been composed during the *puja* festival. The towering pandals remind us of attempts of man to embrace the heights of heaven. But with the absence of the dear mother this pandals have been standing lonely. The poem is deftly loaded with addressee with ambiguity. It might be someone's beloved or the mother Goddess. It unerringly raise the vision of the primordial mother who is often worshipped during the season of festival in Bengal. The Bengali people are very much swayed and carried away into some ecstasy during the festivals. When the Holy Mother is immersed presently after the festival days, the pandals stand alone reminding us of the departure of the Holy Mother. Whither has fled the visionary gleam the glory and the dream. We cannot but reminisce the poignant memory of the autumnal festivity loud with prayers addressed to the Mother. Perhaps the murmuring river gives a tongue echoing the passions.

Uncertainty lies in the logic of affairs. Life appears to be a journey. One does not know when and where the journey might end. And we are all are attached to the fair of worldly life and we are weary of urban raiments. We look forward to a reverse edition of entropy and we will be stripped of all urban hypocrisy surrendering to the true desire of heart. What could be the true desire of heart? Ego has separated us from the continent of cosmic existence. The poet wants to get rid of the separation of the self from the Supreme self. Now with the advent of reverse entropy the dreams of the tryst with one's Supreme self should be burnt. Happily the poet would sink in someone's dream. Thus altruism will prevail.

Happily I would sink in someone's dream. When we see a dreamer in the dream itself it is undoubtedly curious. Despite that we human beings are seldom left lonely. We are always in company with someone who is drawn to dreams. Valmiki or Shakespeare were dreamers and we dip in the dreams of a Shakespeare or a Valmiki or may be of Shankaracharya. And in the poem we have been transported to a fresh world of dreams conjured by someone else. May be s/he is a philosopher or a painter. Here in this fresh world it rains all the years. And the cloud gently sails across the ravaged land and meandering mellows. In a flash we are transported to where the rains are continuous yet fails to drench or fill. It is rather a strange land wrecked by strife and war inflicting destruction and cruelty. Rains stand for fertility and love. There could be rain of kindness and the rain of melody as well. Joy when too deep becomes a close bosom friend of sadness. The shrill of rain evokes the mystic pain. What could be the rains and the mystic pains? Shelley exclaimed that our sweetest songs are those that tell us of the saddest thoughts. And earlier our poet doffed his self to identify himself with the countless souls that crowd the existence. It metamorphoses into an aeolian harp that might respond to every vibration that is generated by the countless atoms. The notes thereof generated by numerous hearts heaving measureless groans might have transformed into a shrill melody of over mind rhythm. The cosmic song or who knows the music of the spheres lulls the poet into sleep. The poet presently wishes that darkness had dropped. He becomes rid of all his pretensions taking refuge under the wings of the Holy Ghost. The widening wings now shed ineffable kindness. And the soul finds its solace in candid confession. What should be the material of the confession? Our beings are laden with desire, anger, lust, craving for power and jealousy. Unburdened self of one is redeemed when we surrender to nature. We are now listening to the heartfelt song of one who has been redeemed and transformed into the spirit of love and compassion.

It is rain. And the rains are moonlit. And the wind is shining silvery when the moon's glimmering gold with blighted eyes gazes upon the earth. Does it find the world wrecked with harrowing sorrow? Often we are fond of dreams. But the poem betakes the traditional route of aesthetics. And the protagonist is worn with dreams. This is a curious expression. As long as awake we participate in battles, blood sheds and triumphs as well as fruition. Here the poet retires from everyday commotion. And night is there with dishevelled hair and the poet hides himself into the darkness with his dream worn eyes. Because he cannot espy the existence loaded with things that engross his senses. With the advent of sleep the poet is plunged into nothingness. In other words the poet attains the measureless monody of thoughtlessness. That is the state of being into a trance and we wakes up in response to cosmic awareness which sings an elegy in the face of transitoriness of the existence.

The sky ripped suddenly apart from end to end to bless the poet. That is what happened to Dante. After having crossed the Purgatorio Dante became face to face with Beatrice standing at the gate of heaven. The sky went apart to bless the poet with an unbound torrent of rain and thunder. As a poem is quite different. And the poet expects torrent and thunder as soon as the gates of heaven are ajar? We are all denizen of desert. We have drunken deep the venom of Inferno. Now destiny showers manna of blessings. It brings life and vigour to the aridity of existence. We prayed for rains and love so that the barren heart of the earth and Nature could be soothed with divine compassion. The dark lady of Shakespeare's Sonnets does not desire that the dried earth should be called back to life again. But that is appearance only. The poem reminds us that the dark matter or dark lady overcomes her apparent ire. She rejoices with the variegated vernal verdure that signifies a deluge of life force sweeping away everything whatever that stands in the way of Eros or life force. Does it echo the Upanishads—Honey blows the wind… Honey oozes from the seas.

www.ingramcontent.com/pod-product-compliance
Lightning Source LLC
Chambersburg PA
CBHW031242130726
47988CB00008B/3205